The Life of
St George

Anita Ganeri

Heinemann
LIBRARY

H **www.heinemann.co.uk/library**
Visit our website to find out more information about **Heinemann Library** books.

To order:
☎ Phone 44 (0) 1865 888066
📄 Send a fax to 44 (0) 1865 314091
💻 Visit the Heinemann Bookshop at www.heinemann.co.uk/library to browse our catalogue and order online.

First published in Great Britain by Heinemann Library, Halley Court, Jordan Hill, Oxford OX2 8EJ, part of Harcourt Education.
Heinemann is a registered trademark of Harcourt Education Ltd.

Editorial: Lucy Thunder and Helen Cannons
Design: Richard Parker and Tinstar Design Ltd. (www.tinstar.co.uk)
Illustrations: Maureen Gray
Picture Research: Rebecca Sodergren and Liz Moore
Production: Edward Moore

Originated by Repro Multi-Warna
Printed and bound in China by South China Printing Company
The paper used to print this book comes from sustainable resources.

ISBN 0 431 18082 2
08 07 06 05 04
10 9 8 7 6 5 4 3

British Library Cataloguing in Publication Data
Anita Ganeri
The Life of St George. – (Life of saints)
270.1'092
A full catalogue record for this book is available from the British Library.

Acknowledgements
The publishers would like to thank the following for permission to reproduce photographs: Art Archive p 18; Bridgeman Art Library p 20; Bridgeman Art Library/Louvre, Paris p 10; Collections/Roger Scruton p 11; Corbis UK Ltd/Bettmann p 23; Corbis UK Ltd/National Gallery, London pp 13, 14; Corbis/Benjamin Rondel p 9; E & E Picture Library/S.C.Clark p 5; Sonia Halliday Photographs pp 22, 24; Sonia Halliday Photographs/Laura Lushington p 15; Sonia Halliday Photographs/David Silverman p 21; Robert Harding Picture Library/Michael Short p 7; Robert Harding Picture Library/Roy Rainford p 25; Mary Evans Picture Library p 12; PA Photos p 27; Rye and Battle Observer p 26; Scala Art Resource pp 6, 19; Skyscan p 17; Topham Picturepoint p 4.

Cover photograph of St George, on a stained-glass window in the Church of St Foy in Conche, France, reproduced with permission of Sonia Halliday Photographs and Laura Lushington.

The publishers would like to thank Fr. Martin Ganeri OP for his assistance in the preparation of this book.

Every effort has been made to contact copyright holders of any material reproduced in this book. Any omissions will be rectified in subsequent printings if notice is given to the publishers.

Contents

Words shown in the text in bold, **like this**, are explained in the glossary.

What is a saint?

In the **Christian** religion, people try to live a **holy** life. Some men and women are especially holy. The Christian Church calls them saints. Christians believe that saints are very close to God.

Some Christians pray to the saints to help them.

Some saints look after a country or a group of people, such as doctors or travellers. They are called **patron saints**. This book is about St George, the patron saint of England.

St George is usually shown as a **knight** in armour.

St George is born

George was born in Turkey, about 1700 years ago. We do not know very much about his life. Most of the information we have comes from stories and legends.

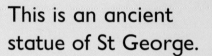

This is an ancient statue of St George.

George came from a wealthy family. We do not know if he had any brothers or sisters. His parents were **Christians**. George learned about being a Christian from a young age.

George was born in Cappadocia, in Turkey, shown here.

Moving home

When George's father died, he and his
mother left their home in Turkey. They
travelled to **Palestine** to live on a large
farm which his mother owned.

Today, Palestine is part of the modern country of Israel. In George's time, it was ruled by the Romans and was part of the mighty Roman Empire.

Palestine, where George lived as a young boy.

A brave soldier

Later, George joined the Roman army and became a soldier. Soon he was given an important job in the army. Legend says that he was very brave and strong.

This sculpture shows a group of soldiers in the Roman army.

News of George's **courage** reached the **emperor**. He called George to see him and gave him a job as one of his guards. George became one of the emperor's favourite soldiers.

These men are dressed like soldiers in the Roman army.

The fierce dragon

A famous story about George's life tells of a fire-breathing dragon. It lived in a marshy swamp near a city in Libya. People were terrified of the terrible beast.

George rode through Libya on his horse.

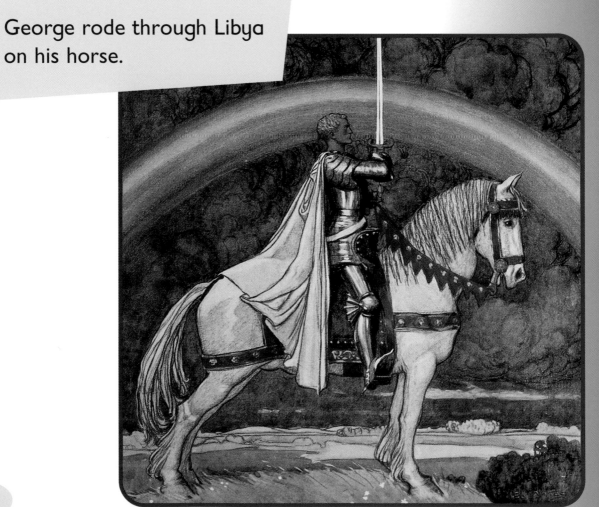

No one could kill the fierce dragon. So every day the people gave it two sheep to eat, to keep it away. Sometimes the dragon ate a person instead.

The dragon was very fierce and always hungry.

Killing the dragon

One day, it was the turn of the king's daughter to be fed to the dragon. Bravely, she went down to the swamp and waited. Just then, George came riding by.

This painting shows the king's daughter waiting for the dragon to eat her.

When George heard the girl's sad story, he promised to help her. He charged at the dragon and killed it with his **lance**. The people and the city were safe at last.

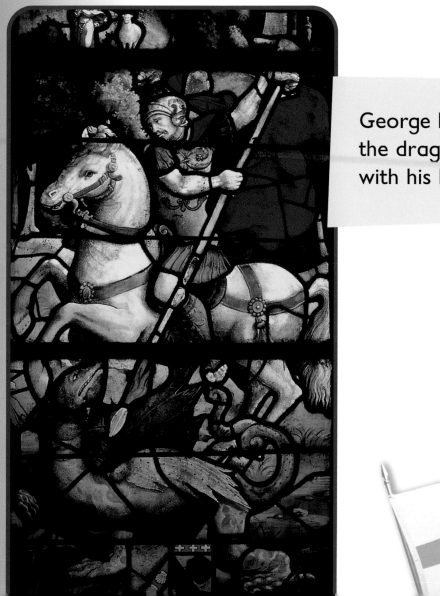

George killing the dragon with his lance.

George's reward

The king was delighted to have his daughter back. He gave George lots of money and jewels. George did not keep them. Instead, he shared them out among the poor and talked to them about God.

George stayed in the city to teach people about being a **Christian**. Many of them became Christians after hearing George speak. Then George jumped on his horse and rode away.

Some stories say that the dragon lived in England. This is Dragon Hill, Oxfordshire.

Dragon Hill

Turning to God

Back in **Palestine**, life was very hard for the **Christians**. The Roman **emperor** wanted them to worship the Roman gods instead. Some Christians were even killed because of their beliefs.

The Romans captured the Christians and killed some of them.

When George saw what was going on, he gave up his soldier's job. He gave away all his money and belongings. From now on, he wanted to do God's work.

This carving shows George praying to God.

George dies

In a fit of temper, the **emperor** had George thrown into prison. He ordered George to give up his **Christian** beliefs. But George refused to do what the emperor wanted.

George's head was chopped off by the emperor's men.

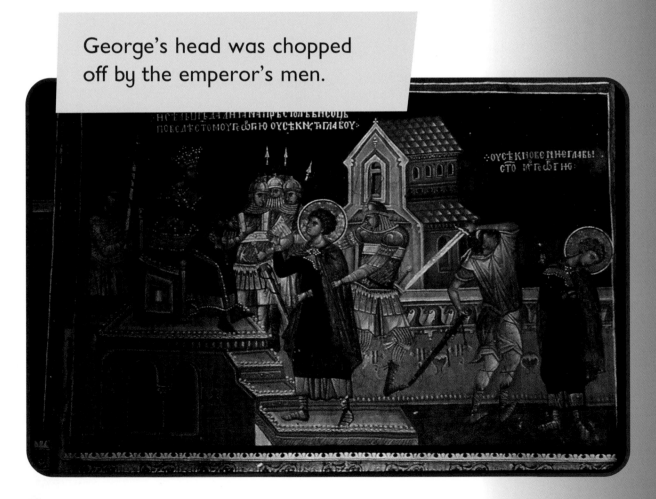

The emperor decided to punish
George. He was cruelly **tortured**, but
he prayed to God to make him strong.
Then he was dragged through the city
and had his head chopped off.

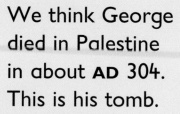

We think George
died in Palestine
in about AD 304.
This is his tomb.

A lucky sign

About a thousand years ago, **Christian knights** from Europe travelled to **Palestine**. They fought against the **Muslims** to try to win back the holy city of Jerusalem.

This carving shows George leading the Christian knights into battle.

The English knights were led by King Richard I. A story tells how, one day, the king saw a **vision** of George. The king won the next battle he fought.

This painting shows Richard I and his knights in a battle.

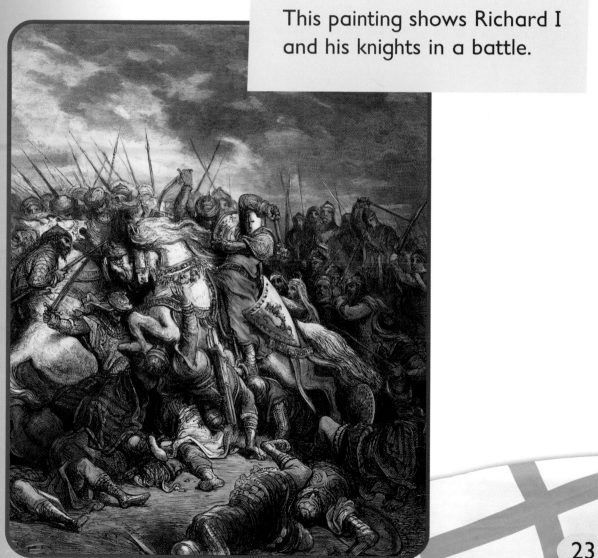

George of England

George was famous for helping to look after people and giving money to the poor. He was also a brave soldier. This is why he was chosen as the **patron saint** of soldiers.

St George's Church in Fordingham, Dorset, is named after George.

We do not know if George ever visited England. But his fame spread far and wide. About 700 years ago, he became the patron saint of England.

This is St George's Chapel at Windsor Castle. The castle is one of the Queen's homes.

St George's Day

On 23 April, people celebrate St George's Day. This is the day on which George died. In some places in England, there are street parades and people wear red roses.

Many people take part in St George's Day parades.

People also fly English flags. In the middle of the English flag is the red cross of St George. This cross appeared on George's armour and his shield.

The flag of England shows the red cross of St George.

Fact file

St George is usually shown as a **knight** in armour, riding on horseback. He carries a white flag with a red cross and a sword or **lance** for killing the dragon.

St George is also the **patron saint** of Germany, Portugal, boy scouts, farmers, archers, horses and armour-makers.

Legend says that, when George killed the dragon, he gave the princess a red rose. On 23 April, in Barcelona, Spain, boys give their girlfriends red roses. St George is also the patron saint of this part of Spain.

In England, one of the highest awards for bravery is a medal called the George Cross. On one side is a picture of St George killing the dragon.

Timeline

We do not know for certain when St George was born or died. You can use the dates below as a guide.

Around AD 270 St George is born in Cappadocia, Turkey

Around 304 St George is killed in Lydda, **Palestine** on 23 April

1189 King Richard I leads the English knights on the Third **Crusade**

1222 St George's Day is celebrated for the first time

Around 1348 King Edward III of England makes St George the patron saint of England

Around 1415 St George's Day began to be celebrated with a great feast

Glossary

AD way of counting years, starting from year zero. This is when some people believe Jesus was born.

Christians people who follow the teachings of Jesus Christ

courage another word for bravery

Crusade war fought between the Christians and the Muslims hundreds of years ago

emperor ruler of the Roman Empire

holy to do with God

knight soldier from hundreds of years ago who wore armour and rode on horseback

lance long, pointed weapon

Muslims people who follow the religion of Islam

Palestine ancient country in the Middle East. Today, much of Palestine is called Israel.

patron saints saints who have a special link to a country or a group of people. A patron is someone who looks after other people.

tortured hurt or injured in a very cruel way to make a person change their mind

vision seeing a vision of something means seeing something that is not really there

Find out more

Books

Celebrations!: Christmas, Jennifer Gillis (Raintree, 2003)

George and the Dragon, and other saintly stories, Richard Brassey (Orion, 2003)

Places of Worship: Catholic Churches, Clare Richards (Heinemann Library, 1999)

Places of Worship: Protestant Churches, Mandy Ross (Heinemann Library, 1999)

Websites

www.britainexpress.com
Information about different parts of Britain, the history of Britain and famous people, including saints.

Index

Titles in *The Life of* series include:

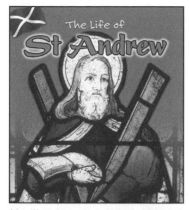

Hardback   0 431 18084 9

Hardback   0 431 18081 4

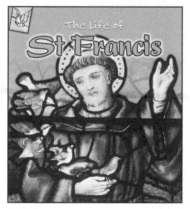

Hardback   0 431 18080 6

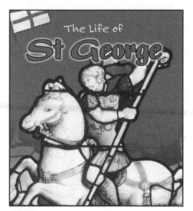

Hardback   0 431 18082 2

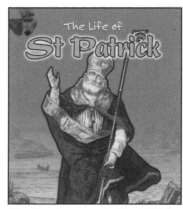

Hardback   0 431 18083 0

Find out about the other titles in this series on our website www.heinemann.co.uk/library